PRAYING
THE
ANGELUS

PRAYING
THE
ANGELUS

The Message of the Angel to Mary

Jean Fournée

Translated by
Robert R. Barr

A Crossroad Book
The Crossroad Publishing Company
New York

The Crossroad Publishing Company
481 Eighth Avenue, New York, NY 10001

Original edition: *Histoire de l'Angélus:*
Le message de l'Ange à Marie,
Pierre Téqui, éditeur

English translation and supplements
to the original French edition copyright © 2000
by The Crossroad Publishing Company

Printed in the United States of America

Library of Congress Cataloging-in-Publication Data

Fournée, Jean.
   [Histoire de L'Angelus. English]
   Praying the Angelus : the message of the angel to Mary / Jean
Fournée ; translated from the French by Robert R. Barr.
     p. cm.
   Includes bibliographical references.
   ISBN 0-8245-1864-0 (alk. paper)
   1. Angelus. I. Title.
BX2175.A48 F6813 2000
242'.74 – dc21

                                     00-009447

1 2 3 4 5 6 7 8 9 10   06 05 04 03 02 01 00

Contents

Foreword

While researching in Florence, Italy, as recently as last year, I was asked by more than one non-Italian friend, and indeed by more than one colleague who thought I might know something about such things, what the significance of the bells that rang in the city periodically throughout the day might be. They had noted the sound, which was haunting and hard to miss — a threefold sequence of three strokes followed by a peal, echoing from numerous belfries — and they had noted, too, the apparently unpredictable timing of the ringing, which did not correspond consistently with the hour or the half hour or anything else. What they were hearing were the bells sounding the Angelus, inviting people to stop for a few minutes wherever they stood, in the morning, after the midday mass, and at dusk, to recollect the mystery of the angel's message to Mary and the saving event of Christ's Incarnation.

My friend's questions highlighted a disjunction that is only too real within much of the devotional life that today's Catholics have inherited from the past: the traditions are mysteriously resonant, and offer a window into an ancient and valued spirituality, but are at the same time achingly hollow to many. The Angelus bells still have the power to catch the attention of those unawares and to make them pause if only for a moment, wondering particularly when perceived as a foreign experience by those who find themselves listening to a foreign culture; but for all their power, the bells' meaning, and the entreaty they press, is as muted to many today as their sound can be pervasive.

The Angelus is a centuries-old prayer sequence, combining the Ave Maria with other Annunciation texts that recall the pivotal event in salvation history when Christ took flesh from Mary, our Mother in Faith, who opened the portal of grace by her humble acquiescence to God's will; it ends with a supplication asking God to open our minds to a recognition of what Christ's Incarnation and Passion has won for us. Formulated first in the thirteenth century, the Angelus could be seen as a time-bound creation reflecting the religious sensibilities of an age when Marian devotion had been given new prominence. Medieval spirituality, guided first by Cistercian monks and then by Franciscan and Dominican friars, had discovered the power of an affective response to the human dimension of the story of Christ's coming and dwelling among us. In the realm of Marian piety this led to a new focus on the earthly life of the Virgin, fostered most especially in confraternities devoted to Mary in which her role as Mediatrix and humble co-sufferer was preached and her praises sung nightly. The Angelus was born in this historical context, certainly, but its message is not only of the past.

The Angelus is a living prayer, which the current pope has made a prominent part of his own devotional praxis, and which today can still offer Christians a means of accessing the reality of the Incarnation through contemplating afresh, and with immediacy, daily, the angel's message to Mary and a young girl's response to her God. But it is a means of access available only if we understand the meaning of the bells that call us to recollect and ask us to pray. Jean Fournée's modest volume has performed the great service of explaining the Angelus and its history. He has thereby helped to recover this traditional prayer's affective power for modern readers. Here is a lesson in how the Church's ancient spirituality, redolent and resonant and still present in our midst, can be made to speak again.

M. MICHÈLE MULCHAHEY
Department of Theology
Fordham University

Introduction

It is astonishing that, since the emergence of unprecedented interest among scholars of ethnosociology, ecclesiology, and the history of Christian devotion in the popular forms of religious belief and practice, so little attention has been given to the Angelus. Yet, in the history and repertory of rites and prayers, the Angelus has been among the most popular. This popularity is due, above all else, to the daily ringing of the bells of our churches. To "sound" the Angelus has certainly more meaning and resonance than to "pray" the Angelus. Moreover, who does not know the celebrated and frequently reproduced tableau of Millet, which appears on our cover? It represents surely the prayer of the Angelus. In looking at it, we know that we are beholding a scene of prayer. But what prayer? Who can recite it exactly, even among practicing Catholics? It is worth recalling here its verses.

What is unusual is that there is no mention of the Angelus either among scholars of folklore or among historians. For the former, the Angelus is not folklore, and yet the very popular character of the Angelus seems also to have evaded the latter, who ignore it altogether in their regional studies devoted to religious practice yesterday and today. This ignorance is surely not new. In 1978, for example, the Society of the History of Normandy published a work entitled *Hier, une chrétienté? Les archevêques de Rouen visitent leur diocèse* ("Yesterday, a Christianity? The archbishops of Rouen visit their diocese"). Here we have a questionnaire sent in 1876 by Cardinal de Bonnechose to all pastors of the diocese of Rouen. Significantly, not one question referred to the ringing or practice of the Angelus. And yet there are 218 questions, referring to the smallest details of the liturgy, the ceremonies, the parish institutions, the church, the school, the cemetery — in a word, everything that concerned the life of the locale.

By contrast, a questionnaire just as precise, just as detailed, and just as probing, sent by Bishop d'Aquin of Sées to the pastors of his diocese in

1701, asks them in no. 26 of the First Article: "how many bells" in the belfry; "whether they can be heard by the whole parish," and "whether they are rung daily in the morning, at noon, and in the evening for the Angelus" (Archives de l'Orne, G 1045).

In 1959, the *Revue de la Manche* ("Channel review") published under the title "Petites gens du Cotentin à la fin du XIXe siècle" ("Humble folk of the Cotentin at the close of the nineteenth century"), contains absolutely authentic recollections, edited by Madame Edith Languille, concerning a family of modest artisans and farmers of the environs of Coutances. The lay schoolteacher of the village, a product of the normal school of Saint-Lô, never failed to have her pupils recite the Angelus before dismissing them at noon. This occurred around 1890. In how many Catholic schools is the Angelus still recited? In how many churches is it still sounded?

And yet, the Angelus is well suited in its rhythm and its schedule for punctuating the Christian's day. It acquired this function gradually over the past several centuries, as it gradually became en-

riched and, at the same time, a factor for the spiritual enrichment of the faithful. It began as an
evening prayer, a prayer of curfew (not that its
ringing is to be confused with the ringing of the
curfew). Then it also became a morning prayer, and
finally a prayer of morning, noon, and evening.

From the start, it is a prayer in praise of the
Blessed Virgin (the three Hail Marys). Then on the
basis of the greeting of the angel it is a meditation
on the mystery of the Incarnation, an introduction
to the mystery of the Redemption, and an assertion of the mediating role of Mary the Mother of
the incarnate Word.

Returning three times a day, from dawn to dusk,
the Angelus acquires the role of making time sacred
or, more precisely, of summoning persons to sanc-
tify it. Hence the significance of sounding the bells.
Bishop d'Aquin's concern was that it should be au-
dible throughout the territory of a parish, so that
all parishioners would be called to pray at the same
hour, with the same words, as if they had been gathered together physically. The monastery bell calls
the religious to celebrate the hours of the canonical
or monastic office. That of the parish church plays

a somewhat similar role, except the space in which the inhabitants of the parish live is more vast than that of the monasteries, and the people are less assiduous in prayer than the monks. Hence, the bell or bells of the church have a role not only of call, of convocation, and of notice, but also of association, or even of substitution. Even where they have become, as Père Paris wrote, "the only voice that speaks of God,"[1] everything must be done so that this voice can continue to reverberate; gathering to prayer those who no longer know how to pray, reminding them in any case that time is the Lord's, and that we are only its temporary beneficiaries.

The Text of the Angelus

Angelus domini nuntiavit Mariae,
Et concepit de Spiritu Sancto.[2]

> *Ave Maria, gratia plena, Dominus tecum.*
> *Benedicta tu in mulieribus*
>   *et benedictus fructus ventris tui, Jesus.*
> *Sancta Maria, Mater Dei,*
>   *ora pro nobis peccatoribus*
> *nunc et in hora mortis nostrae. Amen.*

Ecce ancilla Domini,
Fiat mihi secundum verbum tuum.[3]

> *Ave Maria, gratia plena…*

Et verbum caro factum est,
Et habitavit in nobis.[4]

> *Ave Maria, gratia plena…*

Ora pro nobis, sancta Dei Genetrix,
Ut digni efficiamur promissionibus
    Christi.

Oremus. Gratiam tuam, quaesumus, Domine, mentibus nostris infunde; ut qui, Angelo nuntiante, Christi Filii tui incarnationem cognovimus, per Passionem ejus et Crucem, ad resurrectionis gloriam perducamur. Per eumdem Christum Dominum nostrum. Amen.

The angel of the Lord declared unto Mary,
And she conceived of the Holy Spirit.

> *Hail Mary, full of grace, the Lord is with you.*
> *Blessed are you among women,*
>   *and blessed is the fruit of your womb, Jesus.*
> *Holy Mary, Mother of God,*
>   *pray for us sinners*
> *now and at the hour of our death. Amen.*

Behold the handmaid of the Lord,
Be it done to me according to your word.

> *Hail Mary, full of grace . . .*

And the Word was made flesh,
And dwelled among us.

> *Hail Mary, full of grace . . .*

Pray for us, most holy Mother of God,
that we may be made worthy of the promises
    of Christ.

Let us pray. Pour forth, we beseech you, O Lord, your grace into our hearts, that we to whom the Incarnation of Christ your Son was made known by the message of an angel, may by his Passion and Cross be brought to the glory of his Resurrection. Through the same Christ Our Lord. Amen.

One

Scriptural Antecedents

We find the two gospel references to the Angelus in Saint Luke and in Saint John. However, the mystery of the Annunciation and that of the Incarnation of the Word, thus proclaimed, have their roots in the prophetic visions of the Hebrew Scriptures. At the moment when the waiting is over, at the moment when the promise is accomplished, a good many biblical texts come to the surface, and the messianic light is projected through them. These textual associations are valid not only in their meaning, but in their very form.

The Angel of the Lord carries the message to Mary

The Latin word *Angelus* comes from the Greek *aggelos* (in which the double gamma was pronounced *ng*), meaning "messenger," and the Greek

The most detailed account of the Annunciation comes from the Gospel of Luke (1:26–45):

In the sixth month the angel Gabriel was sent from God to a city of Galilee named Nazareth, to a virgin betrothed to a man whose name was Joseph, of the house of David; and the virgin's name was Mary. And he came to her and said, "Hail, O favored one, the Lord is with you!" But she was greatly troubled at the saying, and considered in her mind what sort of greeting this might be. And the angel said to her, "Do not be afraid, Mary, for you have found favor with God. And behold, you will conceive in your womb and bear a son, and you shall call his name Jesus. He will be great, and will be called the Son of the Most High; and the Lord God will give him the throne of his father David, and he will reign over the house of Jacob for ever; and of his kingdom there will be no end." And Mary said to the angel, "How shall this be, since I have no husband?" And the angel said to her, "The Holy Spirit will come upon you, and the power of the Most High will overshadow you; therefore the child to be born will be called holy, the Son of God. And behold, your kinswoman Elizabeth in her old age has also conceived a son; and this is the sixth month with her who was called barren. For with God nothing will be impossible." And Mary said, "Behold, I am the handmaid of the Lord, let it be to me according to your word." And the angel departed from her.

In those days Mary arose and went with haste into the hill country, to a city of Judah, and she entered the house of Zechariah and greeted Elizabeth. And when Elizabeth heard the greeting of Mary, the babe leaped in her womb; and Elizabeth was filled with the Holy Spirit and she exclaimed with a loud cry, "Blessed are you among women, and blessed is the fruit of your womb! And why is this granted me that the mother of my Lord should come to me? For behold, when the voice of your greeting came to my ears, the babe in my womb leaped for joy. And blessed is she who believed that there would be a fulfillment of what was spoken to her from the Lord."

verb *aggelein*, meaning "to announce." Angels play
a frequent role in the Bible. Among other functions,
they are the emissaries of the will of God.

The one who comes to Mary is called Gabriel by
Saint Luke: It is he who, six months before, had
been sent to Zechariah to foretell the birth of John
the Baptist. It is Gabriel as well who had been sent
to Daniel to explain his vision, and the meaning of
a prophecy found in Deuteronomy 8:9. Let us note
that the angel Gabriel — whose name means "man
of God" or "strength of God" — having informed
Mary of the unexpected pregnancy of her cousin
Elizabeth, added: "Nothing is impossible for God."
These same words had once constituted a comment
on the equally late and unexpected pregnancy of
Sarah, spouse of Abraham (Gen. 18:14).

The angel Gabriel is sent as a messenger, as an am-
bassador of God to Mary. In *The Annunciation* (see
plate 1) of Rogier Van der Weyden (1400–1464),
we see him coming down from heaven and surprising Mary in the privacy of her dwelling, more
precisely on her knees in her room, busied with
reading her psalter, as we read in the *Meditationes
vitae Christi* ("Meditations on the life of Christ"),

1. *The Annunciation.* Rogier Van der Weyden. Alte Pinakothek. Munich, Germany. Foto Marburg/Art Resource, New York.

> *Today angels have become modern again. For years they have held a modest place in theology and general awareness, but today in countless books they are once again treated with respect. In the Bible angels are God's messengers. They indicate that God is at hand to help and heal. They are heralds of another, deeper reality for human beings.*
>
> *Saint Benedict was convinced that monks sing the psalms in the sight of God's angels. They do not sing alone. Angels stand around them and open heaven to their song. Angels bear their prayers to God. Angels tell us: God is near. You are bathed in his healing and loving presence.*[5]

a little Franciscan book well known to the artists of the end of the Middle Ages. The angel sometimes holds his blossoming staff of a messenger or herald of the Lord in his left hand, as proof of his mission and of his divine delegation. His right hand defines a gesture that we often see more explicitly in other works and is related, of course, to his message.

And she conceived of the Holy Spirit

Indeed the Holy Spirit is there, in the form of a dove. Sometimes the dove seems borne by a ray of light shining straight into Mary's face.

In a good many works of this era, especially in the alabaster sculptures, the ray penetrates the ear of the Blessed Virgin, who actually bends her head to the side to receive it, as if mindful of the verse of Psalm 45, "Hear, O daughter, consider and incline your ear" (v. 11). We should not seek a literal reference to one of the apocryphal gospels of the Infancy: "The Word of God penetrated her by her ear,...and thus began the pregnancy of the Holy Virgin." The important thing is the symbol. In fact, the correlation between Eve listening to the tempter and his message of death, and Mary whose attentive ear receives the message of life has been commented upon innumerable times by the Fathers of the Church. Let us recall this passage from the Gospel according to Saint Luke (11:27–28): To the woman who cried, "Blessed is the womb that bore you . . . !" Jesus replied, "Blessed rather are those who hear the word of God and obey it." This,

after all, is the scripture text most apposite here —
this homage rendered Mary by her divine Son.

Behold the handmaid of the Lord

In the designation "handmaid of the Lord" we
have the parallel between Mary and the mother
of Samuel. How often Samuel's mother proclaims
herself the handmaid of the Lord! And when she
gives thanks to him for the birth of her son, the
canticle she improvises has been justly called the
"prototype of the Magnificat": "My heart exults in
the Lord; my strength is exalted in my God..."
(1 Sam. 2:1).

In his *Court traité de théologie mariale* ("Short
treatise on Marian theology"), Abbé René Lau-
rentin has aligned each of the verses of the
Magnificat (according to the original Greek of
Saint Luke's Gospel) with the biblical texts that
may have inspired them, especially the Psalms. Far
from making the Canticle of Mary a sort of kaleido-
scopic conglomeration of biblical reminiscences,
these references actually give the passage its
cohesion, its harmony, its light, and make it appear

Mary recites her song of praise (Luke 1:46–55), the famous Magnificat, which is modeled on Hannah's song of praise in the Hebrew Scriptures (1 Samuel 2):

Mary said, "My soul magnifies the Lord, and my spirit rejoices in God my Savior, for he has regarded the low estate of his handmaiden. For behold, henceforth all generations will call me blessed; for he who is mighty has done great things for me, and holy is his name. And his mercy is on those who fear him from generation to generation. He has shown strength with his arm, he has scattered the proud in the imaginations of their hearts, he has put down the mighty from their thrones, and exalted those of low degree; he has filled the hungry with good things, and the rich he has sent away empty. He has helped his servant Israel, in remembrance of his mercy, as he spoke to our fathers, to Abraham and to his posterity forever."

as it is — a veritable symphony of convergences predestined to what Père Lagrange calls "the great work of mercy promised to Abraham" and realized in her who is the "daughter of Zion" in whom God has chosen to reside.

Be it done to me according to your Word

The representational art of the Romanesque era is so sober in decor and presentation that it frequently seems reduced to simple dogmatic statements — congealed ideograms from which all life seems excluded. Thus, the Annunciation is limited to setting Mary and the angel Gabriel in each other's presence, immobile before each other, as Mary and her cousin Elizabeth will be in the scene of the Visitation.

Indeed, regarding the Annunciation, one can follow the evolution of the scene merely by observing the attitude of the hands of the angel and the Blessed Virgin. Beginning in the thirteenth century, when art became more detailed and picturesque, the scene of the Annunciation represented not a simple evangelical reference, but a "story."

Distracted as one may be by all of the narrative context, the architectural surroundings, the landscape, and by other subjects that threaten to divert attention from the essential to the accessory, a certain set of gestures permits the beholder to follow the development of the events and the dialogue between the messenger from heaven and the "annunciated" Virgin.

One can follow perfectly the development of the conversation merely by attending to the attitude of Mary's hands. They express her states of soul, which begin with surprise, even fear, then move to reticence, to protest, and finally to acceptance, with two climactic moments: when her palms are turned outward, the hands signify not refusal, but protest; when her palms are turned inward, they signify acquiescence, the *Fiat*. At this moment of the *Fiat* Mary crosses her hands on her breast (see plate 2 on the following page).

And the Word was made Flesh

At the end of the Middle Ages and in the Renaissance, there is often enough a little naked child in

2. *Annunciation.* Giusto di Ravensburg, detail of Mary. S. Maria di Castello, Genoa, Italy. Alinari/SEAT/Art Resource, New York.

the ray of light shining from God the Father to the Blessed Virgin: Christ coming to take flesh (see plate 3 on the following page). At times he carries a cross on his shoulder, and sometimes also other instruments of the Passion. The final purpose of both the Annunciation and the Incarnation is clearly expressed: Christ becomes a human being for the redemption of the world. He will be born of Mary to suffer on the cross one day. This Word made flesh is the *Verbum salutiferum* ("salvation-bearing Word," in the words of Rotulus of Ravenna, fifth century). On one manuscript painting of the fifteenth century, Jesus bears his cross and says, "Ecce ego venio cito, merces mea mecum est" (Rev. 22:12): "See, I am coming soon; my reward is with me, to repay according to everyone's work."

Here, too, we have a reminder that Mary will be the mother of the divine crucified one. Surely, the best commentary on this image is simply this verse taken from our Profession of Faith: " . . . and for our salvation he came down from heaven; by the power of the Holy Spirit he was born of the Virgin Mary and became man."

Ad matutinum Versus.

D Omine labia mea aperies. ℞. E t
os meum annunciabit laudē tuā.
℣. Deus in adiutoriū meū intēde
℞. Dñe ad adiuuādū me festina.
Gloria patri, & filio, & spiritui sā
cto. Sicut erat in principio, & nunc, & semper,

3. Annunciation, left side. Hours for Rome use. Colored woodcut, printed in Paris, January 17, 1525, by Simones de Colines for Geoffroy Tory (c. 1480–1533), PML17588, fol. D3v. The Pierpont Morgan Library, New York/Art Resource, New York.

And dwelled among us

Saint John's text echoes that of Exodus (25:8): "And have them make me a sanctuary," said the Lord to Moses, "so that I may dwell among them." The invisible presence of God in the Old Covenant has been replaced by his visible presence in the incarnation of the Word in Mary. She is the first reference of what the same Saint John says in Revelation apropos of the future Jerusalem: "See, the home of God is among mortals" (21:3).

And this goes back to Ezekiel: "I...will set my sanctuary among them forever" (37:26). This is far more than the spiritual presence of the divine Wisdom, evoked for example in Sirach 24:7 or Baruch 3:38. It is the "tangible" presence of the Word become a human to "lead the human being to himself." Père Louis Bouyer claims in *Le Quatrième évangile* ("The Fourth Gospel," Casterman, 1955), that in the text of Saint John, the glory and the dwelling are associated: "We have seen his glory." He, who is regarded by some as one of the three privileged apostles of the Transfiguration, could testify to that glory. He knew the role played by the

4. Annunciation from *Book of Hours* by Jean Poyet (fl. 1450–1500), Tours, France, c. 1500. The Pierpont Morgan Library, New York/Art Resource, New York.

luminous cloud, the sign of the invisible presence of God among the Hebrews. "By the incarnation," writes Père Bouyer, "the inaccessible light is attained." Thus, "the effect of the incarnation has been for us: the dwelling of God in our midst, the vision of his glory."

Two

The Angel's Salutation and the Homage of Elizabeth

Hail Mary

Ave, Maria...Ave means *Salve, Salus!* "Health and Salvation! Good day!" This prayer is known as the "angelic salutation" because of the wish of *salus* (total well-being) implied in this heartfelt greeting.

Is this the correct translation? It is as far as the Latin is concerned. But the corresponding Greek word, *kaire,* (imperative of the verb *kairein*) is much richer. It includes along with the idea of *salus* that of joy and of blessing. "Rejoice, God protect and bless you!"

These words recall the proclamation of the prophet Zephaniah to Israel (Zeph. 3:14): "Sing aloud, O daughter of Zion!" — a messianic message with its echo and fulfillment in the angel's words to Mary.

The oldest of all the Marian prayers echoes in some way the Our Father, since the former, too, is in the Gospel. Indeed, it is chronologically anterior to the Magnificat.

Full of grace

It would be impossible to meditate too long on the dogmatic significance of this phrase. In a missal of the thirteenth century (preserved in the Municipal Library of Rouen), the initial *G* of the introit *Gaudeamus* ("let us rejoice") for the feast of December 8 is illuminated with a miniature representing the "angelic salutation." This is surprising, since December 8 is the feast of the Immaculate Conception of Our Lady. The painter (or the theologian who guided the painter) was six centuries ahead of the bull of Pius IX. In *Ineffabilis Deus* (1854) we read that this fullness of grace (*gratia plena*) permits the assertion that Mary "has never been subjected to the curse, but has, with her Son, shared a perpetual blessing."

Pius IX, whose pontificate was the longest in church history (1846–78), became head of the church at a stormy time. With his bull *Ineffabilis Deus* (1854), Pius decided the question of the Immaculate Conception, which even the Council of Trent (1545–63) had left open.

To the honor of the holy and indivisible Trinity, to the adornment and distinction of the Virgin and Mother of God ... we declare, proclaim, and define that the doctrine which maintains that the most Blessed Virgin, from the first moment of her conception, through the unique grace and preference of almighty God in view of the merits of Jesus Christ ... was preserved from every stain of original sin, was revealed by God and hence is to be believed firmly and constantly by all believers. . . . .

The Lord is with you

This is the wish of Boaz to the reapers: "The Lord be with you" (Ruth 2:4). But here the wish is realized, and we cannot avoid recalling two texts from the Hebrew Scriptures, messianic texts par excellence, that of the prophet Zechariah, "Shout aloud, O daughter of Jerusalem! Lo, your king comes to you" (9:9) and that of the prophet Zephaniah, "Sing aloud, O daughter of Zion, shout, O Israel. Rejoice and exult with all your heart, O daughter of Jerusalem!...The king of Israel, the Lord, is in your midst" (3:14–15).

Blessed are you among women, and blessed is the fruit of your womb, Jesus

Elizabeth's salutation, subsequent to that of the angel Gabriel, also has its biblical antecedents. Thus, we read in the Book of Judges: "Most blessed of women be Jael!" (5:24). But the closest relationship is with the enthusiastic praise reserved for Judith, who saved Israel: "Blessed be you among all peoples....Blessed be you by the Lord Almighty!" (Jud. 14:7, 15:10).

Until the end of the Middle Ages, Elizabeth's salutation, in keeping with Saint Luke's text, ended at *ventris tui* (your womb). It is uncertain when and by whom the name of Jesus was added. It has been

5. *The Visitation:* by Domenico Ghirlandaio (1448–94). Detail of Saint Elizabeth and the Virgin. Louvre, Paris. Giraudon/Art Resource, New York.

said that it was an initiative of Pope Urban IV. What is certain is that the addition "Jesus" appeared in a Carthusian *Rosarium* of the fifteenth century, in which each of the fifty Aves is followed by a christological commentary. For example, after the first Ave we can read, in Latin: "...whom you have conceived of the Holy Spirit, at the announcement of the angel Gabriel."

This salutation by Elizabeth is undoubtedly the first human recognition of the role Mary plays as mediator. It is through the Virgin Mary that Elizabeth becomes aware of the mystery of God becoming human. For the first time, other than by the prophecies, the place of Mary in the plan of redemption is proclaimed upon earth. And it is then that John receives the Holy Spirit — he who was to give testimony to the Light.

Holy Mary, Mother of God, pray for us sinners now and at the hour of our death

Recourse to the intercession of the Virgin occurred very early, perhaps earlier in the East than in the West. This has been verified with the discovery

The "visitation" that Luke reports describes the visit of Mary with Elizabeth. Both are pregnant. Elizabeth will shortly give birth to John the Baptist.

Mary stayed three months with Elizabeth. Like so many women, Mary too became more beautiful in her pregnancy. In body, spirit, and soul she was changed by these months in the mountains with Elizabeth. The song that Mary sang at her meeting with her motherly friend is sung again and again. Even today it speaks about the land of freedom.

> *My soul elevates the Lord,*
> *and my spirit rejoices in God my Savior.*
> *My soul seeks the land of freedom,*
> *and my spirit will come forth*
> *from intimidation.*
> *The empty faces of the women*
> *will be filled with life,*
> *and they will become human beings.*
> *From generations before us,*
> *the sacrificed ones awaited.*

6. *The Visitation,* by Fra Angelico (ca. 1387–1455). Diocesan Museum of Cortona, Italy. Scala/Art Resource, New York.

in 1938 of a fourth-century papyrus bearing the Greek text of the prayer popularized in Latin as the "Sub Tuum Praesidium," which is attributed to Saint Ephrem, the Syrian, who lived at that time. The prayer contains the expression, "O Mother of God," which was current among the Doctors of Alexandria, and most notably Saint Cyril, one of the theologians who achieved the solemn proclamation of the divine motherhood at the Council of Ephesus in 431.

Furthermore, the invocation "Holy Mary, pray for

One important and especially eloquent praiser of Mary was Ephrem the Syrian, whose hymns to Mary were translated from the Syriac and disseminated everywhere. He died in 373. He is considered the author of the first of "Mary's complaints." In his hymns about the Nativity he also touches on the mother-son issue.

The following hymn shows how Ephrem described the way Christ made himself small in order to be born from Mary:

Lest he confuse the onlookers by his greatness,
He reduced himself,
from the universe into the land of the Hebrews,
and from this country to Judea,
and from there to Bethlehem,
till he filled only the little womb (of Mary).

us" must have welled up in the hearts of the faithful long before its inclusion in the Litany of the Saints by Pope Sergius I, at the end of the seventh century. At the time, this invocation was sung in processions on the four Marian feasts.

> *From the eighth to the thirteenth centuries there were only four officially recognized feasts of Mary, and even today, except in the Reformed Churches, they are considered liturgical feasts:*
>
> > *February 2: Mary's Purification*
> > *March 25: Annunciation*
> > *August 15: Mary's Assumption*
> > *September 8: Mary's Birthday*

In the Carolingian "Prayers" studied by Père Barré, we find expressions like, "Holy Mary, pray for us," "Intercede for me, a sinner," or "Succor me on the day of my death."[6]

However, the link between the angelic salutation and the invocation was still long in coming. The liturgy, for the time being, was content with the antiphonal formula. It was essentially through private prayer that the union was made. From the thirteenth century, the formulas of intercession became more precise and varied. It is quite possible that the pious practice of the Fifteen Joys, a prelude to the Rosary inaugurated in the thirteenth century,

With the political upswing of France in the twelfth century, the French Church also took over the religious leadership in the West. Its chief spokesperson was Bernard of Clairvaux (1090–1153). His Cistercian order soon wrested supremacy from the monks of Cluny, who had become highly secularized, and through Bernard it became the great power of the twelfth-century church. Bernard was a great preacher. Moreover, he was an important poet. Here is one example of his Marian poetry:

> *I greet you, Mary full of grace,*
> *the Lord is with you!*
> *With you is the Father,*
> *who makes his Son yours.*
> *With you is the Son,*
> *who in a wonderful mystery*
> *hides in your motherly womb.*
> *With you is the Holy Spirit,*
> *who sanctifies you*
> *with the Father and the Son.*
> *Truly, God is with you, Mary.*

Hildegard of Bingen (1098–1179) composed about seventy spiritual songs, which she set to music herself. Among her *Carmina* we find this prayer (originally in Latin):

> *O bright Mother of sacred healing,*
> *through your holy Son*
> *you have poured oil of anointing*
> *on the wound and woe of death,*
> *which Eve brought us to our misery.*
> *You have annihilated death*
> *and built up new life.*
> *Pray for us to your Son,*
> *Mary, Star of the Sea!*
> *You mediator of life,*
> *you bliss full of splendor,*
> *you sweetness of all joys,*
> *of which you lacked none.*

developed the practice of following each Ave with a prayer of petition. A manuscript of the fourteenth century, for example, provides a text of this prayer, "Come to my aid at the hour of my death."[7]

In the following century, Saint Bernardine of Siena does not hesitate to have "Sancta Maria, ora pro nobis peccatoribus," "Holy Mary, pray for us sinners," appended to "ventris tui," "your womb" (see S. Bernardini, *Opera*, 4:226–27). The Latin formula was complemented in the sixteenth century with the "nunc et in hora mortis nostrae" ("now and at the hour of our death").

Final prayer

"Pour forth, we beseech you, O Lord, your grace into our hearts, that we to whom the Incarnation of Christ your Son was made known by the message of an angel, may by his Passion and Cross be brought to the glory of his Resurrection."

The invocation that introduces the final prayer of the "pious practice" of the Angelus repeats, in a way, that which concludes the Ave Maria, and is found in the liturgical prayer at Rome at the time of Pope Sergius I at the end of the seventh century.

This prayer, the "Gratiam Tuam," it should be noted, is a kind of condensation of the formulas concluding the fifty Aves of the *Rosarium* such as

It was not until Sergius I (687–701) that a pope dealt officially with Mary's status. Admittedly, he did not proclaim a dogma, but he did organize feasts and processions for the major Marian holy days. On the feast of the Assumption, Sergius himself went barefoot as he led a group of believers in Rome from the Lateran to the church of Santa Maria Maggiore — a custom that was not discarded until Pope Pius V did so in 1566.

it was known in the fifteenth century. After the words "Jesus Christ," one of the mysteries of the Rosary, from the Annunciation to the reign of glory, is evoked. The angel's proclamation is found in the final formula of the first Ave, and the glory of the resurrection in that of the last.

Three

A Brief History
of the Angelus

The origins of the Angelus are linked clearly to the spread of the Ave Maria as a private prayer. The Ave, we recall, contained initially only the salutation of the angel Gabriel and that of Elizabeth, according to the text of Saint Luke (1:28, 42):

> Greetings, favored one!
> The Lord is with you.
> Blessed are you among women,
> And blessed is the fruit of your womb.

The Marian legends and miracle tales, which enjoyed great popularity in the twelfth and thirteenth centuries, testify to the extent to which the recitation of the angelic salutation had spread among the faithful. Furthermore, the devotees of the Blessed

Mechthild of Hackeborn, and her sister, Gertrude of Helfta, who wrote down her visions, were nuns of the Cistercian convent of Helfta in Eisleben, and both were contemporaries of the German mystic Mechthild of Magdeburg. She greeted Mary in the *Liber specialis gratiae* with these words:

> *Hail, Mary, with that reverence with which God the Father greeted you by his Ave and in his almighty power freed you from all guilt.*
>
> *Hail, Mary, with that love with which the Son in his wisdom illuminated you and made you the brightest star of heaven and earth . . . .*

Virgin apparently even accompanied each Ave with a genuflection, which could very well be a reflection of the iconographic evolution of the theme of the Annunciation. In the Romanesque era, the angel and Mary stand facing each other. In the thirteenth century, the angel genuflects before her.

This, too, is the age in which the practice of reciting the Ave Maria three times spreads. It is believed that Saint Anthony of Padua (1195–1231) earnestly recommended it. Furthermore, it appears in a special way in the *Revelations* to Mechthild of Hackeborn (1241–98).

Finally, the recitation of these three Aves after Compline in the evening, accompanied by a meditation on the mystery of the Incarnation, is said to have been proposed by Saint Bonaventure on the occasion of a Chapter of the Order of Friars Minor in 1269.

These traditions show that the institution of the pious practice of the Angelus occurred gradually, and that we must wait several more decades before it adopts the form attributed to it by M. Olier.[8] For now, we note only the point of departure in the daily recitation of the three Ave Marias.

The Angelus as first an evening prayer

Saint Bonaventure is said to have taken particular care in 1269 to have the bell rung to call his religious and the faithful of the region to recite the three Aves after Compline. From the start, the prayer was associated with the ringing of the bell. It even seems that, at the convent of the Friars Minor of Arezzo, it was preceded by the anthem, "Angelus locutus est Mariae" ("The angel spoke to Mary").

The practice inaugurated by Saint Bonaventure remained in place for some time. In the fourteenth and fifteenth centuries, the testimonials are numerous and in agreement. At Lerida, in Catalonia, in 1308, the bell was rung three times at dusk for the Angelus "post completorium" ("after Compline"). The same usage prevailed in the Franciscan convents of the province of Venice. At the same time, in Hungary, the evening Aves were also said to the sound of the bell. In 1314, Pope Clement V, sojourning at Carpentras with his Curia, asked that the bells of the Ave Maria be rung there after the singing of Compline. His successor, John XXII, approved by an act of October 13, 1318, the practice of the evening Angelus in the diocese of Saintes. He introduced it in Avignon and granted an indulgence to the faithful who, hearing the bell, would kneel and recite three Ave Marias.

On May 7, 1327, the same John XXII (then seventy-eight years of age) wrote his vicar at Rome ordering him to introduce the same custom there (kneeling and reciting three Aves at the sound of the evening bell) and to attach an indulgence. This was also the provision of the mini-council held at Paris in March 1344 by the archbishop of Sens. In the presence of five bishops, the thirteenth and final canon recommended the practice of the Angelus at the end of each day. Not surprisingly, the same pious usage is attested in very many other places at this time: in 1334 at Tréguier, in 1336 in Hainaut, in 1370 at Nantes, in 1378 in the diocese of Mayence, and so on. As their inscriptions indicate, bells were even specially cast for the ringing of the Angelus.

The evening Angelus and the curfew

Quite a few councils were held in Normandy at the time of William the Conqueror, who was pleased to convoke them and even preside at them. Such was the case at Caen in 1061, where the duke was assisted by Archbishop Maurille of Rouen and Lanfranc, then prior of the Abbey of Bec. It was here that a curfew throughout the duchy was instituted, described simply as a police regulation. Through the dispositions taken in 1047 at the "council" of Vaucelles (a region of Caen), the young duke, who had just triumphed over an armed coalition, took care to apply the Peace of God and the guarantees of safety and security for his subjects. Then at Caen in 1061, it was decided that, in all localities of the duchy the bell would ring each evening to invite the folk to prayer, after which they were to withdraw to their houses and lock their doors. At the same time, new measures were taken to restrict those who would commit thefts and assaults.

This information led to the theory of a connection between the origin of the sounding of the curfew and that of the Angelus, inasmuch as the Angelus was originally only an evening prayer. In actual fact, the prayer or prayers in question at Caen in 1061 were not those of the Angelus, and the ringing of the bells at the end of Compline in the monasteries had nothing to do with a curfew. However, what can be claimed with good reason is that the peal following the discontinuous ringing of the Angelus may be a relic of the old medieval curfew.

What is specific to the Angelus, however, is not the sounding of the peal, but the triple ringing of three strokes preceding it. Originally, the intervals between the three groups of three strokes were supposed to give time to recite the three Aves. This was the case with the Carthusians of the fourteenth century. In the fifteenth century, the Benedictines of the Bursfeld reform, who had 180 monasteries in Germany, Belgium, Holland, and Denmark, performed the custom, at the end of Compline and after a Pater Noster, Ave, and Credo, of prostrating themselves and reciting three Aves at the ringing of the bell. At the same time the canons regular of Windesheim did the same after singing the anthem to the Blessed Virgin.

Among the historical proofs against the association between the ringing of the Angelus and the sounding of the curfew is one reported by W. Henry of England. It concerns the city of Wells, in Somerset. In 1331, one Goddeley, the dean of the chapter, ordered the sounding of three strokes at three short intervals on the great cathedral bell, in order that three Aves might be recited, and this only shortly prior to the curfew. Incidentally, it should be noted that the recitation of the angelic salutation seems to have spread earlier in England than on the Continent. The same is the case also with other aspects of Marian piety.

The morning Angelus

From the fourteenth century onward, it is not surprising to see in England the evening Angelus being complemented with a morning one. This first occurred in the monasteries at the hour of Prime. The secular communities then imitated the monasteries. However, certain variations crept into the content and intentions of the Marian prayer. In 1346, the bishop of Bath, in Somerset, ordered the clergy of his cathedral to recite five Aves morning and evening for benefactors living and dead. In 1399, the archbishop of Canterbury, Thomas Arundel, invited the bishop of London to repeat the evening ringing in the morning, and to have a Pater Noster and five Aves recited at this moment by the clergy and the faithful.

The morning "doubling" of the evening bell and of the three Aves had already been adopted at Pavia in 1330. In addition, a council was held in 1368 at Lavaur (Tarn) in France and was attended by thirteen bishops and presided over by Geoffroi de Vairolles, archbishop of Narbonne. This council prescribed the daily morning recitation of five Paters in memory of the Five Wounds of Christ and seven Aves to recall the Seven Sorrows of Mary. Certainly, this morning prayer, though announced by the bell, is no longer etymologically an Angelus. However, it is interesting to note the association, in 1368, of the devotion to the Seven Sorrows of Our Lady with the devotion of the Five Wounds of Our Lord. Throughout this century this aspect of Marian piety clearly develops an association between the Blessed Virgin and the Passion of Christ. It is in this century that we see the spread of the *Speculum humanae salvationis*, of hymns to the Seven Sorrows of Mary, and the admirable "Salve Mater Dolorosa."

The Angelus did not become fixed in an immovable formula. We shall see this with its extension to the middle of the day, when it adopts the triple daily frequency it has preserved ever since.

7. Pietà. Southeastern Germany, c. 1390. Overpainting from nineteenth century. St. Elizabeth, Marburg, Germany. Foto Marburg/Art Resource, New York.

The midday Angelus

It seems that the midday Angelus, introduced at Olmütz (today Olomouc, in the Czech Republic) in 1413, and at Mayence and Cologne in 1423, was first limited to Friday and concerned only the devotion to the Passion of Christ. By contrast, in

> *The idea of the mother grieving for her son is primordial and can be traced back to Sumerian culture in the third millennium B.C. In the Christian East there was a Good Friday ritual mourning centered around Mary as early as the sixth century, and a similar liturgy was created in the West in the ninth or tenth century. But not until the Crusades, that is, from the early twelfth century onward, was regular devotion to the Mater Dolorosa brought from the East to the West, first to Italy, then to France, England, Holland, and Spain. It reached its high point in the fourteenth century, as pilgrims streamed to the Holy Land.*

1451 the bell was rung daily at the monastery of the Val des Ecoliers at Mons in Hainaut. In 1456, Pope Calixtus III, whose major concern was to respond to the Turkish threat, prescribed a crusade of prayers and asked that the bells be sounded three times a day, with the recitation each time of three Paters and three Aves. The victory of

In the eighth century Eastern monks fled from Iconoclasts in Constantinople and brought the devotion to the Immaculate Conception to the West. In the tenth and eleventh centuries it made its way to England.

This doctrinal issue was not decided for the Catholic world by papal authority until the nineteenth century. It has nothing to do with the problem of virginity, although that was and is a common misunderstanding. The "Immaculate Conception" does not mean that Jesus was born of a virgin, but that, when she was conceived by her parents, Mary herself was exempted from original sin.

Belgrade (1456) saved Christianity momentarily, but the Turks remained redoubtable and menacing.

In 1472, King Louis XI prescribed the extension of the noontime Angelus to all of his kingdom and asked that the intention of the prayers offered be for peace. Hence the name of the midday Angelus as "the Ave Maria of Peace." This practice of the midday Angelus was granted an indulgence in 1475 by Pope Sixtus IV — a great Marian pope, who very especially fostered liturgical devotion to the Immaculate Conception.

From this time onward, the triple Angelus, with its triple bell, can be attested throughout practically all the West: at Beauvais, at Tournai, at Liège, at Aix-la-Chapelle, in England, and so on. Furthermore, Pope Alexander VI, who was far from being a saint, nevertheless confirmed in 1500 the dispositions of Calixtus III.

For the Carthusians, to these three ringings of the Angelus was added a fourth: a nocturnal Angelus, which was recited at the sounding of the bell after the office of Lauds.

•

Abbé Decorde, a historian of the region of Bray, reports a custom inspired by the Angelus that concerns the nuns of the monastery of Clair-Ruissel of the order of Fontevrault, at Gaillefontaine (province of Seine Maritime). On the occasion of a storm, a sister would run through the convent ringing a little bell and repeating, "Et verbum caro factum est" ("And the Word became flesh"), to which the other nuns would respond with an Ave Maria (*Histoire du canton de Forges*, p. 173).

In his doctoral thesis (1986) on Guillaume Briçonnet (1470–1534), Canon Michel Veissière reports an interesting observation made in 1620 by Guy Bretonneau, a genealogist of the Briçonnet family. Bretonneau draws attention to a bull of February 27, 1517, issued by Pope Leo X, granting indulgences "to all those who shall devoutly say a Pater Noster and an Ave Maria when they hear the bell ring for this purpose morning, evening, and midday, in the dioceses of Meaulx and Lodesve, and in the outskirts of Sainct Germain des prèz lès Paris." The bull had been granted at the request of the bishop, whose purpose, writes Veissière, was "incontestably, by means of the indulgence, to foster an authentic spiritual renewal centered on Christ suffering in the company of the Virgin Mary." It was a matter of making one of the "popular forms of devotion...available to the most simple," and whose champion was Bishop Briçonnet.[9] We notice that the prayer includes only one Pater and one Ave at each sounding of the bell.

About the same time, one may read an interesting decision under the heading "De Ave Maria Dicenda" ("Saying the Hail Mary"), among the synod statutes of Bishop Antoine d'Estaing (of Angoulême, 1506–23), published in 1972 in the *Mémoires* of the Historical and Archeological Society of la Charente (pp. 259–316). Here is a translation of a passage from the original Latin text: "We grant to all the faithful of our diocese who, at the hour of morning, midday, and Compline, when the bell shall sound, shall kneel to say three Aves, with devotion and compunction for their sins, forty days' indulgence.... This is to be announced by the archpriests, rectors, and vicars at the Sunday Masses."[10]

Kneeling at the ringing of the Angelus is something the Spaniards have never taken lightly. A Picard peasant visiting Compostela observed: "When the Angelus is rung in this country, wherever you are you must kneel. Foreigners are made to do the same, even by force in case of resistance."[11]

Since the sixteenth century

It was in the sixteenth century that the form of the Angelus such as we recite it today was fixed

The text of the Marian antiphon Regina Coeli is attributed to Pope Gregory V, who died in 999. To this day it is sung at certain times of the liturgical year at the end of Compline, the Church's night prayer.

and popularized. We find it in a Little Office of the Blessed Virgin (*Officium Parvum B.M.V.*) published in Rome at the time of Saint Pius V (1566–72), then in the *Manuale catholicorum* ("Catholics' Manual") of Jesuit Saint Peter Canisius (1521–97), printed at Anvers in 1588. The Angelus is also referred to in our books of piety, depending on their date of publication, either by Pope Benedict XIV (September 14, 1742), or by Pope Leo XIII (March 15, 1884). In fact, it was Benedict XIV who prescribed the substitution of the "Regina Coeli" for the Angelus during Eastertide.

On March 25, 1918, the feast of the Annunciation, an Angelus association for those killed in the war was founded at Blois. In his article in the *Dictionnaire pratique des connaissances religieuses,*

8. Coronation of the Virgin. Northern transept, central entrance, pediment. Cathedral, Chartres, France. Foto Marburg/Art Resource, New York.

Abbé J. Bricout reports that in 1921, according to the *Almanach catholique français* ("French Catholic almanac"), the association then numbered some fifty thousand members, and that it had been approved by Pope Benedict XV and recommended by the episcopate.[12] This association received considerable impetus after it was transferred to Versailles and canonically established with the Trappists of 19, rue du Pont-Colbert, on March 13, 1929. Pius XI enriched it with indulgences. This pious work, whose patron feast was fixed as the day of the Annunciation, had a section reserved for children under the age of twelve, the "Benjamins of the Angelus." All of the associates of course committed themselves to the daily recitation of the Angelus.[13]

Today

Every Sunday and feast day John Paul II recites the Angelus with the people of Rome and pilgrims gathered in Saint Peter's Square and introduces this recitation with a Marian homily. Outside Rome, he assiduously maintains this twofold custom (homily and recitation of the Angelus) on his journeys, even on weekdays. Thus, on his journey to Canada in 1984 — September 13 to Halifax and September 16 to Winnipeg — he said: "At this hour of noon, we are gathered in Saint Mary's Cathedral to recite together the prayer of the Angelus. The

Lord invites us *to pause* and, in the company of the Blessed Virgin Mary and of all the saints, to reflect on the mystery of the Redemption, and to raise our voices to praise the Most Holy Trinity."[14]

And in 1990 the Holy Father addressed the crowd before reciting the Angelus at Kigali, on the Ivory Coast: "This prayer, which I recite every Sunday at Rome with the pilgrims who have come to Saint Peter's Square, gives us the opportunity to intensify our spiritual bond with the Virgin Mary, who walks ahead of all the people of God in the pilgrimage of faith."[15]

Four

Making Time Sacred

Until recently, the Angelus was rung three times
a day in all our belfries. Ringing the bells was the
task, a very exacting one, of the sacristan, or the
custos, as he is called in Normandy. The electrifi-
cation of the bells has simplified things, but there
still has to be someone to push the button. How
many belfries have become voiceless, and how sad,
how melancholy, in fact, is their silence! I do not
know how many heads were bowed, how many
hands folded, how many lips murmured the text,
or at least the Aves of the Angelus. But there was
the ringing of the bell that, even for the least de-
vout, did more than merely mark the course of the
day; it furnished that day with a presence and an
appeal. It was a presence of the divine, a call to
prayer, but to a prayer within. For the ringing of the
bell is not only a piece of information in sound; it is

71

> *The story goes that at Domrémy the young Joan of Arc was very sad when Perrin, the bell-ringer, forgot to ring the Angelus in the evening. "That he might be less negligent, Joan promised him hanks of wool from her sheep" (Vloberg, "Notes sur l'Angélus"). The Perrin referred to was a maker of cloth.*

itself a prayer, a liturgical prayer invested with the power of the sacramental.

Let us not forget that the bells of our churches have been consecrated. What is improperly called their baptism is a ritual consecration involving aspersion, anointing, and incensing. The old *Ordo ad signum ecclesiae benedicendum* ("Order for the blessing of the sign of the church") — *signum* refers to the bell, or the *campana* — in usage since the eighth century, was very much simplified in 1961, but it includes three essentials: Psalm 28, in which the *vox Domini,* the "voice of the Lord," is exalted, and Psalms 147 and 150, in which the most vibrant and sonorous instruments of music share in the praise of the Lord. The prayer that closes the ceremony is precisely a synthesis of the mission of the bell, which the celebrant has just incensed: "May the sound of this bell put the enemy to flight, may it invite the faith of the Christian people, may it fill our persecutors with terror, may it strengthen in the Lord the people that it has assembled!"

Is it not particularly true that the bells share in the praise of the Lord when they ring and sound the Angelus? As such, the Angelus, in popular language, is above all the resounding call that comes from our belfries three times a day and, more than simply a call, it represents prayer itself. The prayer is unimaginable without the ringing that introduces it. By contrast, it is easy to imagine it the other way around: that is, only the ringing. We may even wonder how many of the faithful, still having the opportunity to hear the Angelus ring, do not simply content themselves with the ringing.

Bibliography

Barraud. "Les cloches." *Annales archéologiques de Didron* (1858): 54–71.

———. "L'Angélus." *Annales archéologiques de Didron* (1858): 145–49.

Berlière, U. "L'Angélus." *Le Messager des Fidèles* (1887): 64–71.

———. "L'Angélus." *Dictionnaire de Théologie catholique.* Paris: Letouzey, 1903, vol. 1, col. 1278ff.

Bricout, Abbé J. "Angelus." *Dictionnaire pratique des connaissances religieuses.* Paris: Letouzey, 1925, vol. 1, col. 241–43.

Ebertshäuser, C. H., et al. *Mary: Art, Culture, and Religion through the Ages.* Trans. Peter Heinegg. New York: Crossroad, 1998.

Gerberon, Dom. Dissertation on the Angelus. Paris, 1675.

Gruen, A. *Angels of Grace.* New York: Crossroad, 1998.

Henry, W. "Angelus." *Dictionnaire d'Archéologie chrétienne e de Liturgie.* Paris: Letouzey, 1907, vol. 1, part 2, cols. 2068–78.

Longpré, E. "Angelus." *Catholicisme.* Paris, 1948, vol. 1, cols. 554–56.

Mabillon, Dom. *Acta Sanctorum O.S.B.* Paris, 1685, vol. 5, lxxvii–lxxviii.

Matelot, J. "L'Angélus." *Le Bouais-Jan* (periodical of the Cotelin), no. 2 (September 1970): 10–11.

Morineau, B. M. *L'Angélus des Heures douloureuses...et di-*
     vines. Notes catholiques du temps du guerre 30. Langres:
     Imprimerie Saint-Pierre, 1940.
Revue du Clergé français 31 (1902): 24–29.
Thurston, H. "The Angelus." *The Month* 98 (1902): 483–99,
     607–16; 99 (1903) 61–73, 518–32.
Vloberg, M. "Notes sur l'Angélus." *Sanctuaires et Pélerinages*
     7 (1957): 51; also in *Calendrier marial du pélerin* 10
     (1957–58): 18–19.

Notes

Introduction

1. *Dictionnaire pratique des connaissances religieuses* vol. 1 (Paris: Letouzey, 1925), col. 242 .

The Text of the Angelus

2. Luke 1:26.
3. Luke 1:38
4. John 1:14.

Chapter 1: Scriptural Antecedents

5. A. Gruen, *Angels of Grace* (New York: Crossroad Publishing, 1998), 7–10.

Chapter 2: The Angel's Salutation and the Homage of Elizabeth

6. See *Prières anciennes de l'Occident à la Mère du Sauveur* (Paris, 1963), 38.
7. Latin Text in Wilmart, *Auteurs spirituels et textes dévots*, 359.

Chapter 3: A Brief History of the Angelus

8. See *Les grandeurs de Marie d'après les écrivains de l'Ecole française* (Paris: Desclée de Brouwer, 1936), 598–604.
9. *L'évêque Guillaume Briçonnet* (Provins, 1986), 122, 124.
10. I owe this information to the Reverend Canon Veissière.

11. See Bonnalt d'Houet, *Le pèlerinage d'un paysan picard* (Montdidier, 1890), 47–48; cited by Barret and Gurgand in *Priez pour nous à Compostelle* (Hachette, 1978), 130.

12. *Dictionnaire pratique des connaissances religieuses* vol. 1 (Paris: Letouzey, 1925).

13. See François Veuillot, "L'Association de l'*Angélus*," in *Catholicisme*, vol. 1 (Paris, 1948). The Abbey of Sainte-Marie de Versailles (non-reformed Cistercians) no longer exists. Its abbot and several of its religious were of Dutch origin. When the monastery closed, several went to Lérins.

14. John Paul II in Canada, Téqui, 257.

15. Discourse of the Pope, September 9, 1990, Téqui.

OF RELATED INTEREST

Rev. T. Ronald Haney
With illustrations by
Bro. Michael O'Neill McGrath, OSFS
STATIONS OF THE CROSS
The Story of God's Compassion

Evidence dating as far back as the second century A.D.
acknowledges the fact that Christians began this holy
practice from the very earliest times in the Church.
The Stations of the Cross recall the passion and death
of the savior and help us remember the great price
that Jesus paid for our salvation.

0-8245-1769-5; $14.95 (hardcover)

Rev. T. Ronald Haney
With illustrations by
Bro. Michael O'Neill McGrath, OSFS
PRAYERS FOR PRIESTS
And Those Who Pray for Them

A collection of prayers for today's busy priests,
for those who pray for them, and for everyone
baptized into the priesthood of Christ.

0-8245-1816-0; $14.95 (hardcover)

crossroad

OF RELATED INTEREST

Roy Abraham Varghese
GOD-SENT
A History of the Accredited Apparitions of Mary

God-Sent is an overview of the major apparitions of Mary
throughout the course of human history and across the globe.
The book presents evidence in favor of these apparitions,
a study of the messages transmitted at each apparition,
and an inquiry into the nature and meaning of
this global phenomenon.

Varghese presents the scriptural and early Christian literature
to give a plausible, divine origin to the incidents.

0-8245-1843-8; $39.95 (hardcover)

Please support your local bookstore, or call 1-800-395-0690.
For a free catalog, please write us at
THE CROSSROAD PUBLISHING COMPANY
481 EIGHTH AVENUE, SUITE 1550
NEW YORK, NY 10001

We hope you enjoyed Praying the Angelus.
Thank you for reading it.

crossroad